ANCIENT
GREECE

ANCIENT CIVILIZATIONS

ANCIENT
GREECE

Edited by Michael Anderson

Britannica
Educational Publishing
IN ASSOCIATION WITH

ROSEN
EDUCATIONAL SERVICES

Published in 2012 by Britannica Educational Publishing
(a trademark of Encyclopædia Britannica, Inc.)
in association with Rosen Educational Services, LLC
29 East 21st Street, New York, NY 10010.

Distributed exclusively by Rosen Educational Services.
For a listing of additional Britannica Educational Publishing titles, call toll free (800) 237-9932.

First Edition

Britannica Educational Publishing
Michael I. Levy: Executive Editor, Encyclopædia Britannica
J.E. Luebering: Director, Core Reference Group, Encyclopædia Britannica
Adam Augustyn: Assistant Manager, Encyclopædia Britannica

Anthony L. Green: Editor, Compton's by Britannica
Michael Anderson: Senior Editor, Compton's by Britannica
Sherman Hollar: Associate Editor, Compton's by Britannica

Marilyn L. Barton: Senior Coordinator, Production Control
Steven Bosco: Director, Editorial Technologies
Lisa S. Braucher: Senior Producer and Data Editor
Yvette Charboneau: Senior Copy Editor
Kathy Nakamura: Manager, Media Acquisition

Rosen Educational Services
Alexandra Hanson-Harding: Editor
Nelson Sá: Art Director
Cindy Reiman: Photography Manager
Matthew Cauli: Designer, Cover Design
Introduction by Alexandra Hanson-Harding

Library of Congress Cataloging-in-Publication Data

Ancient Greece / edited by Michael Anderson.
    p. cm. — (Ancient civilizations)
"In association with Britannica Educational Publishing, Rosen Educational Services."
Includes bibliographical references and index.
ISBN 978-1-61530-513-1 (library binding)
1. Greece—Civilization--To 146 B.C.—Juvenile literature. I. Anderson, Michael, 1972-
DF77.A5874 2012
938—dc22

                                                                    2011000086

On the cover, page 3: The Poseidon Temple overlooks the Mediterranean from a headland in Sounion, Greece. *Shutterstock.com*

Pages 10, 17, 29, 43, 52, 80 © www.istockphoto.com/Hancu Adrian; pp. 15, 16, 20, 21, 35, 36, 37, 56, 57, 66, 67 ©www.istockphoto.com/Peter Zelei; remaining "interior background images" ©www.istockphoto.com/Alessandro Contadini; back cover shutterstock.com

CONTENTS

When Pericles became leader of Athens around 460 BC, he set out to make it "the queen of Hellas (Greece)." He succeeded. During his 30-year rule, Pericles brought Athens to its greatest glory, making it the most beautiful, brilliant, and powerful city in the Greek world. He had the Acropolis rebuilt with gleaming marble temples to replace those that had been destroyed in war. But more importantly, Athens became an unrivaled center for the arts, mathematics, science, political thought, and philosophy. Some of the most brilliant minds that ever lived—the playwright Sophocles, the sculptor Phidias, and the philosopher Socrates among them—were gathered in one place, reaching for ever higher levels of achievement. As Pericles said, "Our love of what is beautiful does not lead to extravagance; our love of the things of the mind

The Erechtheum , a temple of the goddess Athena, stands atop the Acropolis of Athens, Greece. Six marble female figures, called caryatids, serve as pillars on its famous Porch of the Maidens. Milos Bicanski/Getty Images

does not make us soft." These stubborn, inventive, experimental Athenians helped to lay the foundations of Western civilization.

But there was much more to ancient Greece than Athens. Athens was just one of the many so-called city-states that occupied mainland Greece. And from this peninsula the Greeks spread over a vast collection of islands in the Aegean Sea and to colonies along the coasts of the Mediterranean and Black seas. Unlike most ancient civilizations, Greece wasn't held together by one powerful leader. The city-states were independent, each with its own system of government, and they were just as likely to compete as to cooperate.

There is also much more to ancient Greece's long history than the age of Pericles. In this volume you will discover the great Minoan civilization of Crete, which left behind beautiful art and palaces, and the Mycenaean kingdom, which fought the Trojan War and would later be immortalized in the *Odyssey*. You will also learn about other powerful city-states, such as fierce, militarized Sparta, which united with Athens to defeat the powerful Persian Empire in the early 5th century BC.

You will also see the contentious side of the ancient Greeks. The golden age of Pericles was undone after *hubris*—a Greek word for

exaggerated pride—among the Athenians, combined with the jealousy of other city-states, inspired the momentous Peloponnesian War between Sparta and Athens. The two powers led alliances that, between them, included nearly every Greek city-state. The fighting, which lasted nearly 30 years, ended with the defeat of Athens and the demise of its empire. A more long-range result of the war was the weakening of all the city-states.

The influence of Greece was revived in the 4th century BC by the young Macedonian king Alexander the Great. He established his rule throughout Greece before setting out for world domination, conquering land as far away as India. Through his conquests he spread Greek culture far and wide, a process that continued in the centuries after his death. In Greece itself, the Hellenistic Age, as this era was known, was a time of fine art and sophisticated thought. But Greece never regained its power, and it was defeated by the Roman Empire in 146 BC.

Ancient Greece brought the world plentiful gifts—democracy, geometry, drama, philosophy, and lyric poetry among them. In this volume you will see how the creative, contentious Greeks developed ways of thinking and being that still shape the world today.

9

CHAPTER 1
THE ORIGINS OF
ANCIENT GREECE

"The glory that was Greece," in the words of American writer Edgar Allan Poe, was short-lived and confined to a very small geographic area. Yet it has influenced the growth of Western civilization far out of proportion to its size and duration. The Greece that Poe praised was primarily Athens during its golden age in the 5th century BC. Strictly speaking, the state was Attica; Athens was its heart. The English poet John Milton called Athens "the eye of Greece, mother of arts and eloquence." Athens was the city-state in which the arts, philosophy, and democracy flourished. At least it was the city that attracted those who wanted to work, speak, and think in an environment of freedom. In the rarefied atmosphere of Athens were born ideas about human nature and political society that are fundamental to the Western world today.

Athens was not all of Greece, however. Sparta, Corinth, Thebes, and Thessalonica were but a few of the many other city-states

The Parthenon, the chief temple of the goddess Athena, is the most prominent building on the Acropolis of Athens. **Scott Barbour/ Getty Images**

that existed on the rocky and mountainous peninsula at the southern end of the Balkans. Each city-state was an independent political unit, and each vied with the others for power and wealth. These city-states planted Greek colonies in Asia Minor, in southern Italy and Sicily, and on the coasts of France, Spain, and northern Africa.

MINOAN CIVILIZATION

The islands and mainland of what is now Greece were the site of the earliest civilizations in Europe. The first of these Aegean civilizations—named for the sea that borders Greece—was that of the Minoans, which began on the island of Crete around 3000 BC. The origin of the Minoans is unknown, but by 1600 BC they dominated the Aegean

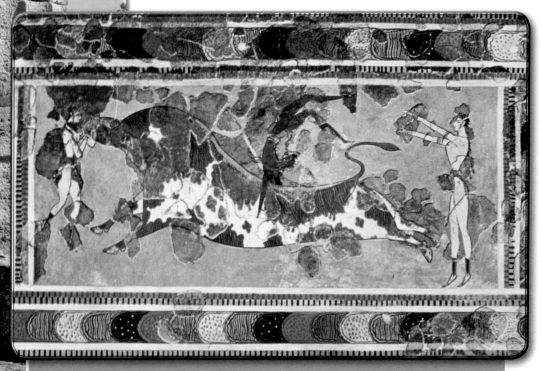

This famous Minoan fresco, depicting a man leaping over a bull, once adorned a wall of the palace at Knossos, Crete. The Bridgeman Art Library/Getty Images

region. Their prosperity depended upon seafaring and trade, especially with the Middle East and with Egypt.

The Minoan civilization is named after the legendary King Minos. According to mythology, Minos was the son of Zeus, the king of the gods, and Europa, a Phoenician princess. The great palace at Knossos, the Minoan capital, covered 5.5 acres (2.2 hectares). Palace ruins show evidence of paved streets and piped water. The palace and the city were protected by a powerful navy. Minoan culture is notable for its use of writing and its fine pottery.

MYCENAEAN CIVILIZATION

The Mycenaeans invaded the Greek mainland from the north beginning in about 1900 BC and conquered the Minoans in about 1400 BC. They are named for Mycenae, their most important city. The Mycenaeans engaged in agriculture, industry, commerce, and war. Their trade routes extended to Sicily, Egypt, Palestine, Troy, Cyprus, and Macedonia.

Mycenaean culture was heavily influenced by that of the Minoans. The Mycenaeans built massive walled cities and

The gold funeral mask of Agamemnon, a heroic Greek king who ruled either at Mycenae or at nearby Argos during the Trojan War. It is displayed in the National Archaeological Museum in Athens. **Silvio Fiore/SuperStock/Getty Images**

made fine goldwork, pottery, and vases. They adapted the Minoan system of writing to create their own language, which is believed to be the most ancient form of Greek. Mycenaean myths and legends lived on through oral transmission into later stages of Greek civilization.

THE TROJAN WAR

The Mycenaeans engaged in many conflicts, but none is more famous than their legendary battle against Troy, a city in Asia Minor (in what is now Turkey). The Trojan War is said to have taken place in the 12th or 13th century BC. It stirred the imagination of the ancient Greeks more than any other event in their history, and it was celebrated in the famous *Iliad* and *Odyssey* by the poet Homer. Yet behind these legends is some truth. There really was a city named Troy, and the stories about the war were based on a struggle between the Trojans and the Mycenaeans for control of trade

The Procession of the Trojan Horse into Troy *by Giovanni Domenico Tiepolo, c. 1760, National Gallery, London.* SuperStock/Getty Images

through the strait called the Hellespont (now the Dardanelles).

In the traditional accounts of the war, Paris, son of the Trojan king, ran off with Helen, wife of Menelaus of Sparta, whose brother Agamemnon then led a Greek expedition against Troy. The ensuing war lasted 10 years, finally ending when the Greeks pretended to withdraw, leaving behind them a large wooden horse with a raiding party concealed inside. When the Trojans brought the horse into their city, the hidden Greeks opened the gates to their comrades, who then sacked Troy, massacred its men, and carried off its women. It is not known for certain how closely this legend reflects actual historical events.

THE DORIAN INVASION

In about 1100 BC Greece was overrun by an invasion of tribes from the north. The Dorians and, later, the Ionians occupied the areas where the Minoan-Mycenaean cultures had flourished. The Dorian invasion swept away the last of the declining Mycenaean civilization and plunged the region into a Dark Age—a time of chaotic movements of tribes in Greece. The Dark Age did not end until the Greek city-states began to emerge almost three centuries later.

CHAPTER 2
THE CITY-STATES

Just as Europe is divided into many small nations rather than a few large political units, so ancient Greece was divided into many small city-states. The term "city-state" is a modern one, coined probably by historian William Warde Fowler in his 1893 book, *The City-State of the Greeks and Romans*. For the Greeks the word was *polis*, which means both "city" and "state." It could as well mean "independent sovereignty." It is the word from which politics, the art of government, is derived. In the 4th century BC the philosopher Aristotle wrote a book entitled *Politics*. It was entirely about the governing of the polis, because he could imagine no other type of sovereignty that could be self-governing.

ORIGINS

The ancient city-states of Greece developed from small villages into moderate-size cities. The type of land strongly influenced the course of development. Greece is a

country of mountains and valleys, making land communication difficult. It was an ideal locale for the growth of completely independent, geographically separated communities.

Sometimes the Greek city-states were separated by mountains. Often,

Ancient Greece.

however, a single plain contained several city-states, each surrounding its acropolis, or hilltop fortress. These flattopped, inaccessible rocks or mounds are characteristic of Greece and were first used as places of refuge. From the Corinthian isthmus rose the lofty acrocorinthus, from Attica the Acropolis of Athens, from the plain of Argolis the mound of Tiryns, and, loftier still, the Larissa of Argos. On these rocks the Greek cities built their temples and their king's palace, and their houses clustered about the base.

Separated by natural barriers and by local pride and jealousy, the various city-states never conceived the idea of uniting the Greek-speaking world into a single political unit. They formed alliances only when some powerful city-state embarked on a career of conquest and attempted to make itself mistress of the rest. Many influences made for unity—a common language, a common religion, a common literature, similar customs, the religious leagues and festivals, the Olympic Games—but even in time of foreign invasion it was difficult to induce the cities to act together.

THE OLYMPIC GAMES

The Olympic Games are considered to have begun in 776 BC, the first year the winners' names were recorded. The popularity of the games was so great that the four-year period between games, known as an Olympiad, became a means of recording time. The games were staged in the wooded valley of Olympia, which was already renowned as a spiritual gathering place and was occupied by great temples dedicated to the gods Zeus and Hera.

An ancient Greek vase dating from about 525 BC depicts Olympic runners. **Picture Post/Hulton Archive/Getty Images**

There are several myths surrounding the origin of the games—both Zeus and the legendary Hercules have been credited with starting the event. According to a poem by Pindar written in the 5th century BC, Pelops created the games in order to celebrate the victory that made him a king.

At first the only Olympic event was the stade, a footrace of about 200 yards (182 meters). Eventually a race twice as long as the stade was added. By 708 BC more racing events had been added as well as wrestling and the pentathlon, a five-part event that included running, wrestling, jumping, and throwing the discus and javelin. In time, boxing, chariot racing, and other events were included. Winners were crowned with wreaths of wild olive branches. Only men were allowed to compete in the games, and only men and certain priestesses were allowed to watch the competitions. A separate sporting festival known as the Heraea was held for female athletes. The original Olympic stadium could seat more than 40,000 spectators. The games were so popular in the ancient world that an *ekecheiria* ("truce") was announced before the start of the games. This truce required that warfare cease in order to allow athletes and spectators safe passage to Olympia. Under Roman rule during the pagan era, the Olympic Games continued to be held for many years. Emperor Theodosius I, however, abolished the games in AD 393.

COLONIES

Only in a few cases did a city-state push its holdings beyond very narrow limits. Athens held the whole plain of Attica, and most of the Attic villagers were Athenian citizens. Argos conquered the plain of Argolis. Sparta made a conquest of Laconia and part of the fertile plain of Messenia. The conquered people were subjects, not citizens. Thebes attempted to be the ruling city of Boeotia but never quite succeeded.

Similar city-states were found all over the Greek world, which had early flung its outposts throughout the Aegean Basin and even beyond. There were Greeks in all the islands of the Aegean. Among these islands was Thasos, famous for its gold mines. Samothrace, Imbros, and Lemnos were long occupied by Athenian colonists. Other Aegean islands inhabited by Greeks included Lesbos, the home of the poet Sappho; Scyros, the island of Achilles; and Chios,

The ruins of a Greek theater in Taormina, Sicily, Italy. **Piotr Malecki/Getty Images**

Samos, and Rhodes. Also settled by Greeks were the nearer-lying Cyclades—so called (from the Greek word for "circle") because they encircled the sacred island of Delos—and the southern island of Crete.

The western shores of Asia Minor were fringed with Greek colonies, reaching out past the Propontis (Sea of Marmara) and the Bosporus to the northern and southern shores of the Euxine, or Black, Sea. In Africa there were, among others, the colony of Cyrene, now the site of a town in Libya, and the trading post of Naucratis in Egypt. Sicily, too, was colonized by the Greeks, and there and in southern Italy so many colonies were planted that this region came to be known as Magna Graecia (Great Greece). Pressing farther still, the Greeks founded the city of Massilia, now Marseilles, France.

Types of Government

The government of many city-states, notably Athens, passed through four stages from the time of Homer to historical times. During the 8th and 7th centuries BC the kings disappeared. Monarchy gave way to oligarchy—that is, rule by a few. The oligarchic successors of the kings were the wealthy landowning nobles, the *eupatridae*, or "well-born." However, the rivalry among these nobles and the discontent of the oppressed masses was so great that soon a third stage appeared.

The third type of government was known as tyranny. Some eupatrid would seize absolute power, usually by promising the people to right the wrongs inflicted upon them by the other landholding eupatridae. He was known as a "tyrant." Among the Greeks this was not a term of reproach but merely meant one who had seized kingly power without the qualification of royal descent. The tyrants of the 7th century were a stepping-stone to democracy, or the rule of the people, which was established nearly everywhere in the 6th and 5th centuries. It was the tyrants who taught the people their rights and power.

ATHENS AND SPARTA

By the beginning of the 5th century BC, Athens had gone through these stages and emerged as the first democracy in the history of the world. Between two and three centuries before this, the Athenian kings had made way for officials called "archons," elected by

The statesman Solon explains his laws to the Athenians. **Archive Photos/Getty Images**

the nobles. Thus an aristocratic form of government was established.

In about 621 BC an important step in the direction of democracy was taken, when the first written laws in Greece were compiled from the existing traditional laws. This reform was forced by the peasants to relieve them from the oppression of the nobles. The new code was so severe that the adjective "draconic," derived from the name of its compiler, Draco, is still a synonym for "harsh." Unfortunately, Draco's code did not give the peasants sufficient relief. A revolution was averted only by the wise reforms of Solon, about a generation later. Solon's reforms only delayed the overthrow of the aristocracy, and in about 561 BC Pisistratus, supported by the discontented populace, made himself tyrant. With two interruptions, Pisistratus ruled for more than 30 years, fostering commerce, agriculture, and the arts and laying the foundation for much of Athens' future greatness.

Very different was the course of events in Sparta, which by this time had established itself as the most powerful military state in Greece. Under the strict laws of Lycurgus it had maintained its primitive monarchical

A statue of Leonidas, king of ancient Sparta, stands over the battle-field of Thermopylae in central Greece. In the battle of Thermopylae, in 480 BC, 300 Spartans under Leonidas fought heroically against the Persians despite overwhelming odds. **AFP/Getty Images**

form of government with little change. Nearly the whole of the Peloponnesus had been brought under its iron heel, and it was now jealously eyeing the rising power of its democratic rival in central Greece.

CHAPTER 3
CLASSICAL GREEK CIVILIZATION

The classical period of Greek civilization corresponds roughly to the 5th and 4th centuries BC. Its start can be dated somewhat earlier, with democratic reforms introduced by the Athenian statesman Clisthenes in about 508 BC. The fledgling democracy was more fully developed under the leadership of Pericles, whose rule represents the pinnacle of Greek civilization. During this time the arts and philosophy reached a level that has rarely been rivaled.

THE PERSIAN WARS

At the start of the classical period, the promising structure of the new Greek civilization was threatened by Persia, the great Asian empire of the day. Persia had been awakened to the existence of the free peoples of Greece by the aid that the Athenians had sent to their oppressed kinsmen in Asia Minor. The Persian empire mobilized its gigantic resources in an effort to conquer Greece. The survival of

Greek culture and political ideals depended on the ability of the small, disunited Greek city-states to band together and defend themselves against Persia's overwhelming strength. The struggle, known in Western history as the Persian Wars, or Greco-Persian Wars, lasted 20 years—from 499 to 479 BC.

Persia already numbered among its conquests the Greek cities of Ionia in Asia Minor. The Persian Wars began when some of these cities revolted against Darius I, Persia's king.

Athenian warriors defeat vastly superior numbers of Persians at the battle of Marathon, in 490 BC. **Hulton Archive/Getty Images**

Athens sent a small fleet to aid the Ionians. After the Persians crushed the revolt, Darius determined to conquer Athens as revenge for its support of the rebels.

In 492 BC Darius sent a fleet across the Hellespont, but the invasion was called off after a storm wrecked his ships. Two years later Darius dispatched a new fleet, and this time his army landed on the plain of Marathon, about 25 miles (40 kilometers) from Athens. Although the Athenians were greatly outnumbered, their daring general Miltiades ordered his force to attack. The battle of Marathon ended with a decisive Greek victory. The Greek historian Herodotus says the Persians lost 6,400 men against only 192 on the Greek side.

Darius planned another expedition, but he died before preparations were completed. This gave the Greeks a 10-year period to prepare for the next battles. Athens built up its naval supremacy in the Aegean under the guidance of Themistocles. This shrewd statesman had seen that naval strength, not land strength, would in the future be the key to power. He persuaded his fellow Athenians to build a strong fleet—larger than the combined fleets of all the rest of Greece—and to fortify the harbor at Piraeus, near Athens.

A Greek fleet defeats much larger Persian naval forces in the battle of Salamis. Time & Life Pictures/Getty Images

In 480 BC the Persians returned, led by Xerxes, the son of Darius. The decisive battle took place in the narrow strait between Piraeus and the island of Salamis. Xerxes' ships outnumbered the Greek ships three to one. The Persians expected an easy victory, but one after another their ships were sunk or crippled. Two hundred Persian ships were destroyed, others were captured, and the rest fled. Xerxes and his forces hastened back to Persia. The battle of Salamis was the first great naval battle recorded in history.

Soon after, the rest of the Persian army was scattered at Plataea (479 BC). In the same year Xerxes' fleet was defeated at Mycale. Although a treaty was not signed until 30 years later, the threat of Persian domination was ended.

ATHENS' RISE TO POWER

From this momentous conflict Athens emerged a blackened ruin yet the richest and most powerful state in Greece. The naval fleet that had defeated the Persians also enabled Athens to dominate the Aegean area. Within three years after Salamis, Athens had united the Greek cities of the Asian coast and of the Aegean islands into a confederacy (called

the Delian League because the treasury was at first on the island of Delos) for defense against Persia. In another generation this confederacy became an Athenian empire.

Almost at a stride Athens was transformed from a provincial city into an imperial capital. Wealth beyond the dreams of any other Greek state flowed into its coffers—tribute from subject and allied states, customs duties on the flood of commerce that poured through Piraeus, and revenues from the Attic silver mines. The population increased fourfold or more, as foreigners streamed in to share in the prosperity. The learning that had been the creation of a few "wise men" throughout the Greek world now became fashionable. Painters and sculptors vied in beautifying Athens with the works of their genius. Even today, these art treasures remain among the greatest surviving achievements of human skill. The period in which Athens flourished, one of the most remarkable and brilliant in the world's history, reached its culmination in the age of Pericles, 460–430 BC. Under the stimulus of wealth and power, with abundant leisure and free institutions, the citizen body of Athens attained a higher average of intellectual interests than any other society before or since.

PERICLES

The "glory that was Greece" reached its height in the 5th century BC, in Athens, under the leadership of the statesman Pericles. He opened Athenian democracy to the ordinary citizen, he built the magnificent temples and statues on Acropolis, and created the Athenian empire.

Pericles. Hulton Archive/Getty Images

Pericles was born in Athens in about 495 BC to a family of wealth and position. His father, Xanthippus, was also a statesman, and his mother, Agariste, was a member of the politically powerful Alcmaeonid family. Pericles himself first gained fame in the spring of 472, when he provided and trained the chorus for Aeschylus' play *The Persians*.

Pericles was first elected *strategos*, or general, in 458. Generals were elected yearly to devise and carry out the strategy necessary to manage the affairs of state at home and abroad. Pericles won reelection for about 30 years. In a time of kings and tyrants as rulers, his policy at home was to place the state in the hands of the whole body of citizens under the rule of law. The Assembly made the laws, the Council of 500 executed them, and popular courts judged those who broke them.

About this time the war with Persia finally ended. Pericles asserted Athenian control over the newly formed Delian League and used its treasury to rebuild the Acropolis, which had been destroyed by the Persians. In 447 work started on the Parthenon, and the sculptor Phidias began work on the statue of the goddess Athena.

Pericles realized his ambition to make Athens, "the queen of Hellas," not only the most beautiful but the most powerful of the Greek states. He lived also to see the states of the Peloponnesus, under Sparta's leadership, rise against Athens' overgrown power in the Peloponnesian War. The closing years of his life were times of storm and trouble. While Athens was besieged by the enemy outside the walls, a terrible plague raged within. For the first time Pericles fell from popular favor and was deposed from office. Only a few weeks later the people repented and reinstated him with greater powers than before. But weakness from an attack of plague killed Pericles the following autumn, in 429.

DAILY LIFE IN THE AGE OF PERICLES

The Athenians led simple lives. They ate two meals a day, usually consisting of bread, vegetable broth, fruit, and wine. Olives, olive oil, and honey were common foods. Cheese was often eaten in place of meat. Fish was a delicacy.

The two-story houses of the Athenians were made of sun-dried brick and stood on narrow, winding streets. Even in the cold months the houses were heated only with a brazier, or dish, of burning charcoal. The houses had no chimneys, only a hole in the

roof to let out the smoke from the stove in the tiny kitchen. There were no windows on the first floor, but in the center of the house was a broad, open court. Clustered about the court were the men's apartment, the women's apartment, and tiny bedrooms. There was no plumbing. Refuse was thrown in the streets.

The real life of the city went on outdoors. The men spent their time talking politics and philosophy in the agora, or marketplace. They exercised in the athletic fields, performed military duty, and took part in state festivals. Some sat in the Assembly or the Council of 500 or served on juries. There were 6,000 jurors on call at all times in Athens, for the allied cities were forced to bring cases to Athens for trial. Daily salaries were paid for jury service and service on the Council. These made up a considerable part of the income of the poorer citizens.

The women stayed at home, spinning and weaving and doing household chores. They never acted as hostesses when their husbands had parties and were seen in public only at the theater—where they might attend tragedy but not comedy—and at certain religious festivals.

SLAVERY

Despite the democratic ideals of Athens, it must be remembered that a very large part of the population was not free, because the Athenian state rested on a foundation of slavery. Two-fifths (some authorities say four-fifths) of the population were slaves. Slave labor produced much of the wealth that gave the citizens of Athens time and money to pursue art and learning and to serve the state.

Slavery in Greece was a peculiar institution. When a city was conquered, its inhabitants were often sold as slaves. Kidnapping boys and men in "barbarian," or non-Greek, lands and even in other Greek states was another steady source of supply. If a slave was well educated or could be trained to a craft, he was in great demand.

An Athenian slave often had a chance to obtain his freedom, for quite frequently he was paid for his work, and this gave him a chance to save money. After he had bought his freedom or had been set free by a grateful master, he became a "metic"—a resident alien. Many of the slaves, however, had a miserable lot. They were sent in gangs to

39

the silver mines at Laurium, working in narrow underground corridors by the dim light of little lamps.

THE PELOPONNESIAN WAR

The growth of Athenian power aroused the jealousy of Sparta and other independent Greek states and the discontent of Athens' subject states. The result was a war that put an end to the power of Athens. The long struggle, called the Peloponnesian War, began in 431 BC. It was a contest between a great sea power, Athens and its empire, and a great land power, Sparta and the Peloponnesian League.

The plan of Pericles in the beginning was not to fight at all, but to let Corinth and Sparta spend their money and energies while Athens conserved both. He had all the inhabitants of Attica come inside the walls of Athens and let their enemies ravage the plain year after year, while Athens, without losses, harried their lands by sea. However, the bubonic plague broke out in besieged and overcrowded Athens. It killed one fourth of the population, including Pericles, and left the rest without spirit and without a leader. The first phase of the

In 413 BC, during the second phase of the Peloponnesian War, the Spartans defeated the Athenian fleet in the harbor of Syracuse. Time & Life Pictures/Getty Images

Peloponnesian War ended with the outcome undecided.

Almost before they knew it, the Athenians were whirled by the unscrupulous demagogue Alcibiades, a nephew of Pericles, into the second phase of the war (414–404 BC). Wishing for a brilliant military career, Alcibiades persuaded Athens to undertake a large-scale expedition against

41

Syracuse, a Corinthian colony in Sicily. The Athenian armada was destroyed in 413 BC, and the captives were sold into slavery.

This disaster sealed the fate of Athens. The allied Aegean cities that had remained faithful now deserted to Sparta, and the Spartan armies laid Athens under siege. In 405 BC the whole remaining Athenian fleet of 180 triremes was captured in the Hellespont at the battle of Aegospotami. Besieged by land and powerless by sea, Athens could neither raise grain nor import it, and in 404 BC its empire came to an end. The fortifications and long walls connecting Athens with Piraeus were destroyed, and Athens became a vassal of triumphant Sparta.

CHAPTER 4
LATE STAGES OF GREEK CIVILIZATION

Sparta tried to maintain its supremacy by keeping garrisons in many of the Greek cities. This custom, together with Sparta's hatred of democracy, made its domination unpopular. At the battle of Leuctra, in 371 BC, the Thebans under their gifted commander Epaminondas put an end to the power of Sparta. Theban leadership was

The tholos (circular building) was built in 393 BC, in Marmaria, Delphi, Greece, 11 years after the end of the Pelopponesian War. **Farrell Grehan/Photo Researchers**

short-lived, however, for it depended on the skill of Epaminondas. When he was killed in the battle of Mantinea, in 362 BC, Thebes had really suffered a defeat in spite of its apparent victory. The age of the powerful city-states was at an end, and a prostrated Greece had become easy prey for a would-be conqueror.

THE RISE OF MACEDON

Such a conqueror was found in the young and strong country of Macedon, which lay just to the north of classical Greece. Its King Philip, who came to power in 359 BC, had a Greek education. Seeing the weakness of the disunited city-states, he made up his mind to take possession of the Greek world. The great orator Demosthenes saw the danger that threatened and by a series of fiery speeches against Philip sought to unite the Greeks as they had once been united against Persia.

The military might of Philip proved too strong for the city-states, and at the battle of Chaeronea (338 BC) he established his leadership over Greece. Before he could carry his conquests to Asia Minor, however, he was killed and his power fell to his son Alexander, then not quite 20 years old.

Young Alexander, later to become the conqueror known as Alexander the Great, listens to his tutor, the philosopher Aristotle. **Stock Montage/Archive Photos/Getty Images**

ALEXANDER THE GREAT

More than any other world conqueror, Alexander III of Macedon deserves to be called the Great. He proved himself to be one of the greatest generals the world has ever known, firmly entrenching his rule throughout Greece and then building up an empire that embraced nearly the entire known world.

In 336, the year he came to the throne, Alexander marched southward to Corinth, where all the Greek city-states (except Sparta) swore allegiance to him. Thebes, however,

Alexander the Great's conquests freed the West from the menace of Persian rule and spread Greek civilization and culture into Asia and Egypt. His vast empire stretched east into India. **Encyclopædia Britannica, Inc.**

later revolted, and Alexander destroyed the city. He allowed the other city-states to keep their democratic governments.

With Greece secure, Alexander prepared to carry out his father's bold plan and invade Persia. In 334 BC he crossed the Hellespont with a Greek and Macedonian force of about 30,000 foot soldiers and 5,000 cavalry. At the Granicus River, in May, he defeated a large body of Persian cavalry, four times the size of his own. Then he marched southward along the coast, freeing the Greek cities from Persian rule and making them his allies.

Alexander's army and a huge force led by Darius III of Persia met at Issus in 333 BC. Alexander charged with his cavalry against Darius, who fled. Alexander then marched southward along the coast of Phoenicia and established his dominance there. Late in 332 BC the conqueror reached Egypt. The Egyptians welcomed him as a deliverer from Persian misrule and accepted him as their pharaoh, or king.

Leaving Egypt in the spring of 331 BC, Alexander went in search of Darius. He met him on a wide plain near the village of Gaugamela, near the town of Arbela (present-day Irbil in Iraq). Although his forces were greatly outnumbered, Alexander again led his

The captive family of Darius III, the defeated king of Persia, kneels at the feet of Alexander the Great following the battle of Issus in 333 BC. Darius had fled during the battle. **Hulton Archive/Getty Images**

cavalry straight toward Darius. Darius fled once more, and Alexander won a great victory. After the battle he was proclaimed king of Asia.

Alexander was determined to press on to the eastern limit of the world, which he believed was not far beyond the Indus River. Throughout Central Asia he founded cities that had many of the features of a Greek polis. This practice began a new chapter in Greek expansion.

In 327 BC Alexander reached India. At the Hydaspes River (now Jhelum) he defeated the army of King Porus. Then he pushed farther east. His exhausted army soon refused to go farther, however, and Alexander reluctantly turned back. He reached Susa, the Persian capital, in 324 BC. The next year he went to Babylon. Long marches and many wounds had so lowered his vitality that he was unable to recover from a fever. He died in 323 BC.

THE HELLENISTIC AGE AND ROMAN CONQUEST

The three centuries after the death of Alexander are called the Hellenistic Age, from the Greek word *hellenizein*, meaning "to act like a Greek." During this period, Greek language and culture spread throughout the eastern Mediterranean world and mixed with the characteristics of the conquered nations. The age was a time of great wealth and splendor. Art, science, and letters flourished and developed. The private citizen no longer lived crudely, but in a beautiful and comfortable house, and many cities adorned themselves with fine public buildings and sculptures.

The Hellenistic Age came to an end with another conquest—that of Rome. On the field of Cynoscephalae, in Thessaly, the Romans defeated Macedonia in 197 BC and gave the Greek cities their freedom as allies. The Greeks caused Rome a great deal of trouble, and in 146 BC Corinth was burned. The Greeks became vassals of Rome. Athens alone was revered and given some freedom. To its schools went many Romans, the future statesman Cicero among them.

When the seat of the Roman Empire was transferred to the east, Constantinople became the center of culture and learning and Athens sank to the position of an unimportant country town. In the 4th century AD Greece was devastated by the Visigoths under Alaric; in the 6th century it was overrun by the Slavs; and in the 10th century it was raided by the Bulgars. In 1453 the Turks seized Constantinople, and within a few years practically all Greece was in their hands. Only in the 19th century, after a protracted struggle against their foreign rulers, did the Greeks finally regain their independence.

Venus de Milo, one of the most famous examples of Hellenistic sculpture, is now in the Louvre Museum, Paris. **Hulton Archive/Getty Images**

CHAPTER 5

ACHIEVEMENTS OF
THE ANCIENT GREEKS

The glorious culture of the Greeks had its beginnings before the rise of the city-states to wealth and power and survived long after the Greeks had lost their independence. The men of genius who left their stamp on the golden age of Greece seemed to live a life apart from the tumultuous politics and wars of their era. They sprang up everywhere, in scattered colonies as well as on the Greek peninsula. When the great creative age had passed its peak, Greek artists and philosophers were sought as teachers in other lands, where they spread the wisdom of their masters.

What were these ideas for which the world reached out so eagerly? First was the determination to be guided by reason, to follow the truth wherever it led. In their sculpture and architecture, in their literature and philosophy, the Greeks were above all else reasonable. The art of the Greeks was singularly free from exaggeration. Virtue was for them a path between two extremes—only by temperance, they believed, could human-kind attain happiness. "Nothing to excess" (*meden agan*) was their central doctrine, a doctrine that the Roman poet Horace later interpreted as "the golden mean."

LITERATURE

Over a period of more than 10 centuries, the ancient Greeks created a literature of such brilliance that it has rarely been equaled and never surpassed. In poetry, tragedy, comedy, and history, Greek writers created master-pieces that have inspired, influenced, and challenged readers to the present day. The Greek world of thought was so far-ranging that there is scarcely an idea discussed today that was not debated by the ancient writers.

POETRY

The earliest Greek literature belongs to the preclassical period. At the beginning of this period stand the monumental epic poems of Homer, the *Iliad* and the *Odyssey*. The figure of Homer is shrouded in mystery. Although the works as they now stand are credited to him, it is certain that their roots reach far back before his time. The *Iliad* is the famous

The disguised Odysseus triumphs over his wife Penelope's suitors by driving an arrow through the blades of 12 axes. **Drawing by Steele Savage**

story about the Trojan War. It centers on the person of Achilles, who embodied the Greek heroic ideal.

While the *Iliad* is pure tragedy, the *Odyssey* is a mixture of tragedy and comedy. It is the story of Odysseus, one of the warriors at Troy. After 10 years fighting the war, he spends another 10 years sailing back home to his wife and family. During his voyage, he loses all of his comrades and ships and makes his way home to Ithaca disguised as a beggar.

Both of these works were based on ancient legends. The stories are told in language that is simple, direct, and eloquent. Both are as fascinatingly readable today as they were in ancient Greece.

The other great epic poet of the preclassical period was Hesiod. He is more definitely recorded in history than is Homer, though very little is known about him. He was a native of Boeotia in central Greece, and he lived and worked in about 700 BC. His two works were *Works and Days* and *Theogony*. The first is a faithful depiction of the dull and poverty-stricken country life he knew so well, and it sets forth principles and rules for farmers. *Theogony* is a systematic account of creation and of the gods. It vividly describes the ages of humankind, beginning with a long-past golden age.

SAPPHO

The dates of her life are uncertain, but Sappho flourished from about 610 to 580 BC. She was one of the best lyric poets of ancient Greece. Unfortunately nearly all of her works have been lost. Except for one work, only fragments have survived. Sappho lived most of her life

Sappho. **Hulton Archive/Getty Images**

in Mytilene on the island of Lesbos, and she is reputed to have married Cercolas from the island of Andros.

The themes of Sappho's poems are personal, concerning friendships and enmities with other women. Her brother Charaxus was also the subject of several poems. She wrote about the loves, hates, and jealousies that flourished among the wealthy women who often met together in associations to spend their days composing poetry and other relaxations. Her poems probably circulated in her lifetime. They were collected during the 3rd or 2nd century BC and published in 10 books. This edition did not survive the Middle Ages. By the 8th or 9th century AD she was represented only by quotations in the works of other authors. Her only surviving complete poem is 28 lines long.

The type of poetry called lyric got its name from the fact that it was originally sung by individuals or a chorus accompanied by the instrument called the lyre. The two major lyric poets were Sappho and Pindar. Sappho has always been admired for the beauty of her writing. She wrote on personal themes. Pindar was born in about 518 BC and is considered the greatest of the Greek lyricists. His masterpieces were the poems that celebrated athletic victories in the games at Olympia,

Delphi, Nemea, and the Isthmus of Corinth. With Pindar the transition was made from the preclassical to the classical age.

DRAMA

The Greeks invented invented drama and produced masterpieces that are still reckoned as drama's crowning achievement. In the age that followed the defeat of Persia (490 to 479 BC), the awakened national spirit of Athens was expressed in hundreds of superb tragedies based on heroic and legendary themes of the past. Greek dramatists were also accomplished in the genre of comedy.

Tragedy

The tragic plays grew out of simple choral songs and dialogues performed at festivals of the god Dionysus. Wealthy citizens were chosen to bear the expense of costuming and training the chorus as a public and religious duty. Attendance at the festival performances was regarded as an act of worship. Performances were held in the great open-air theater of Dionysus in Athens. All of the greatest poets competed for the prizes offered for the best plays.

Of the hundreds of tragedies written and performed during the classical age, only a limited number of plays by three authors have survived: Aeschylus, Sophocles, and Euripides. The earliest of the three was Aeschylus, who was born in 525 BC. He wrote between 70 and 90 plays, of which only seven remain. Many of his dramas were arranged as trilogies, groups of three plays on a single theme. The *Oresteia* (story of Orestes)—consisting of *Agamemnon*, *Choephoroi* (Libation-bearers), and *Eumenides* (Furies)—is the only surviving trilogy. *Persians* is a song of triumph for the defeat of the Persians. *Prometheus Bound* is a retelling of the legend of the Titan Prometheus, a superhuman who stole fire from heaven and gave it to humankind.

Sophocles' life covered nearly the whole period of Athens' golden age. He wrote more than 100 plays, only seven of which remain. His drama *Antigone* is typical of his work: its heroine is a model of womanly self-sacrifice. He is probably better known, though, for *Oedipus Rex* and its sequel, *Oedipus at Colonus*.

The third of the great tragic writers was Euripides. He wrote at least 92 plays, but only 19 still exist in full (including one whose authorship is disputed). His tragedies

Famous British actors Laurence Olivier and Sybil Thorndike play lead roles in a production of Sophocles' tragedy Oedipus Rex *in London in 1945.* Merlyn Severn/Hulton Archive/Getty Images

are about real men and women instead of idealized figures. The philosopher Aristotle called Euripides the most tragic of the poets because his plays were the most moving. His dramas are performed on the modern stage more often than those of any other ancient poet. His best-known work is probably the powerful *Medea*, but his *Alcestis*, *Hippolytus*, *Trojan Women*, *Orestes*, and *Electra* are no less brilliant.

Comedy

Like tragedy, comedy arose from a ritual in honor of Dionysus, but in this case the plays were full of frank obscenity, abuse, and insult. At Athens the comedies became an official part of the festival celebration in 486 BC, and prizes were offered for the best productions.

As with the tragedians, few works still remain of the great comedic writers. Of the works of earlier writers, only some plays by Aristophanes exist. For boldness of fantasy, merciless insult, unqualified indecency, and outrageous and free political criticism, there is nothing to compare to the comedies of Aristophanes. In *The Birds* he held up Athenian democracy to ridicule. In *The Clouds* he attacked the philosopher

61

Socrates. In *Lysistrata* he denounced war. Only 11 of his plays have survived.

During the 4th century BC, there developed what was called the New Comedy. Menander is considered the best of its writers. Nothing remains from his competitors, however, so it is difficult to make comparisons. The plays of Menander, of which only the *Dyscolus* (Misanthrope) now exists, did not deal with the great public themes about which Aristophanes wrote. He concentrated instead on fictitious characters from everyday life—stern fathers, young lovers, intriguing slaves, and others.

HISTORY

Two of the most excellent historians who have ever written flourished during Greece's classical age: Herodotus and Thucydides. Herodotus is commonly called the father of history, and his *History* contains the first truly literary use of prose in Western literature. Thucydides, however, was the better historian. His critical use of sources, inclusion of documents, and laborious research made his *History of the Peloponnesian War* a significant influence on later generations of historians.

A third historian, Xenophon, began his *Hellenica* where Thucydides ended his work about 411 BC and carried his history to 362 BC. His writings were superficial in comparison to those of Thucydides, but he wrote with authority on military matters. He therefore is at his best in the *Anabasis*, an account of his participation in a Greek mercenary army that tried to help the Persian Cyrus expel his brother from the throne. Xenophon also wrote three works in praise of the philosopher Socrates—*Apology*, *Symposium*, and *Memorabilia* (Recollections of Socrates).

Philosophy

The greatest prose achievement of the 4th century BC was in philosophy. There were many Greek philosophers, but three names tower above the rest: Socrates, Plato, and Aristotle. It is impossible to calculate the enormous influence these thinkers have had on Western society. Socrates himself wrote nothing, but his thought (or a reasonable presentation of it) has been preserved in the *Dialogues* of Plato. Even in translation, Plato's style is one of matchless beauty. All human experience is within its range. Best known of the *Dialogues* is the *Republic*, a

Aristotle. **Imagno/Hulton Archive/Getty Images**

fairly long work. There are also many shorter books—such as the *Apology*, *Protagoras*, and *Gorgias*—that contain the penetratingly insightful conversations of Socrates and his friends on every matter relating to human behavior.

In the history of human thought, Aristotle is virtually without rival. The first sentence of his *Metaphysics* reads: "All men by nature desire to know." He has, therefore, been called the "father of those who know."

Aristotle was a student at Plato's Academy, and it is known that—like his teacher—he wrote dialogues, or conversations. None of these exists today. The body of writings that has come down to the present probably represents lectures that he delivered at his own school in Athens, the Lyceum. Even from these books the enormous range of his interests is evident. He explored matters other than those that are today considered philosophical. The treatises that exist cover logic, the physical and biological sciences, ethics, politics, and constitutional government. He also wrote treatises entitled *On the Soul* and *Rhetoric*. His *Poetics* has had an enormous influence on literary theory and has served as an interpretation of tragedy for more than 2,000 years.

SOCRATES

Interested in neither money, nor fame, nor power, Socrates wandered along the streets of Athens in the 5th century BC. Talking to whoever would listen, he asked questions, criticized answers, and poked holes in faulty arguments. His style of conversation has been given the name Socratic dialogue.

Socrates was the wisest philosopher of his time. He was the first of the three great teachers of ancient Greece—the other two being Plato and Aristotle. Today he is ranked as one of the world's greatest moral teachers. His self-control and powers of endurance were unmatched. The young, aristocratic military genius Alcibiades said of him, "His nature is so beautiful, golden, divine, and wonderful within that everything he commands surely ought to be obeyed even like the voice of a god."

Socrates was born on the outskirts of Athens in about 470 BC. He studied sculpture, his father's profession, but soon abandoned this work to "seek truth" in his own way. Socrates shunned the shallow notion of truth for its own sake. He turned to his conscience for moral truth and enjoyed creating confusion by asking simple questions. He sought to uncover the nature of virtue and to find a rule of life. Favorite objects of his attacks were the Sophists, who charged a fee for their teaching. "Know thyself" was the motto he is reputed to have learned from the oracle at Delphi. In knowing oneself he saw the possibility of learning what is really good, in contrast to accepting mere outward appearance.

Socrates, however, was not appreciated by the Athenian mob and its self-serving leaders. His genius for exposing pompous frauds made him many enemies. At last, three of his political foes indicted him on the charge of "neglect of the gods" and "corruption of the young." They were false charges, but politically convenient. In 399 he was sentenced to die by drinking hemlock. His parting comments to his judges were simple, as recorded in Plato's *Apology*: "The hour of departure has arrived, and we go our ways — I to die, and you to live. Which is better God only knows."

The death of Socrates. Hulton Archive/Getty Images

With the death of Aristotle in 322 BC, the classical era of Greek literature drew to a close. In the successive centuries of Greek writing there was never again such a brilliant flowering of genius as appeared in the 5th and 4th centuries BC.

ART

The art of the ancient Greeks, together with that of the ancient Romans, is known as classical art. Classical art owes its lasting influence to its simplicity and reasonableness, its humanity, and its sheer beauty. The first and greatest period of classical art began in Greece in about the middle of the 5th century BC, when artists made great strides in representing the human form.

SCULPTURE

Early Greek statues were stiff and flat, but in about the 6th century BC the sculptors began to study the human body and work out its proportions. They learned to represent the human form naturally and easily, in action or at rest. They were interested chiefly in portraying gods, however. They thought of their gods as people, but grander and more beautiful than any human being. They tried, therefore, to portray ideal beauty rather than any particular person. Their best sculptures achieved almost godlike perfection in their calm, ordered beauty.

The 5th century BC was made illustrious in sculpture by the work of three great masters, all known today in some degree by surviving works. Myron is famous for the boldness with which he fixed moments of violent action in bronze, as in his famous *Discobolus*, or Discus Thrower. There are fine copies now in Munich and in the Vatican, in Rome. The *Doryphorus*, or Spear Bearer, of Polyclitus was called by the ancients the Rule, or guide in composition. The Spear Bearer was believed to follow the true proportions of the human body perfectly.

The greatest name in Greek sculpture is that of Phidias. Under his direction the sculptures decorating the Parthenon were planned and executed. Some of them may have been the work of his own hand. His great masterpieces were the huge gold and ivory statue of Athena that stood within this temple and the similar one of Zeus in the temple at Olympia. They have disappeared. Some of his great genius can be seen

in the remains of the sculptures of the pediments and frieze of the Parthenon. Many of them are preserved in the British Museum. They are known as the Elgin Marbles after the British diplomat Lord Elgin, who brought them from Athens to England in 1801–12.

PAINTING

The Greeks had plenty of beautiful marble and used it freely for temples as well as for their sculpture. They were not satisfied with its cold whiteness, however, and painted both their statues and their buildings. Some statues have been found with their bright colors still preserved, but most of them lost their paint through weathering. The works of the great Greek painters have disappeared completely, and we know only what ancient writers tell us about them. Parrhasius, Zeuxis, and Apelles, the great painters of the 4th century BC, were famous as colorists. Polygnotus, in the 5th century, was renowned as a draftsman.

Fortunately we have many examples of Greek vases. Some were preserved in tombs; others were uncovered by archaeologists at other sites. The beautiful decorations on these vases give us some idea of Greek painting. They are examples of the wonderful feeling for form and line that made the Greeks supreme in the field of sculpture.

The earliest vases—produced from about the 12th century to the 8th century BC—were decorated with brown paint in the so-called geometric style. Sticklike figures of men and animals were fitted into the over-all pattern. In the next period the figures of men and gods began to be more realistic and were painted in black on the red clay. In the 6th century BC the figures were left in red and a black background was painted in.

ARCHITECTURE

The most impressive examples of Greek architecture were temples. Until the age of Alexander the Great, the Greeks erected permanent stone buildings almost exclusively for religious monuments. Their temples were not large enclosures of space but statue chambers containing a god's sacred image. These chambers were accessible only to priests. Yet the Greek temple has always been seen as fundamentally distinct from most other early temples, partly because of the simplicity of its form, partly

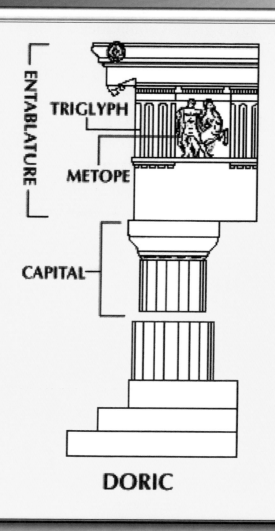

ENTABLATURE

TRIGLYPH

METOPE

CAPITAL

DORIC

Greek architecture developed two distinct orders, or styles — the Doric and the Ionic — and later a variant of the Ionic, the Corinthian. Although each order has characteristic differences in each of its parts, it is the capital (column top) that is most distinctive. Copyright Encyclopædia Britannica, Inc.; rendering for this edition by Rosen Educational Services

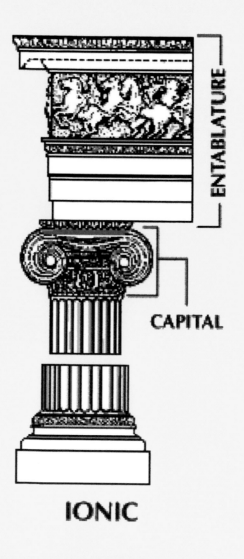

ENTABLATURE

CAPITAL

IONIC

Ionic. Copyright Encyclopædia Britannica, Inc.; rendering for this edition by Rosen Educational Services

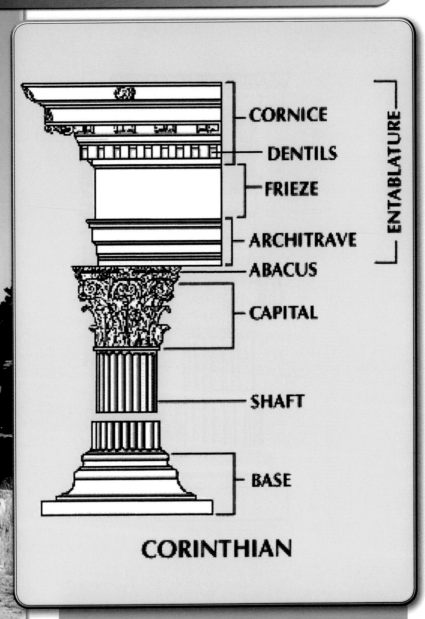

CORNICE

DENTILS

FRIEZE

ARCHITRAVE

ABACUS

CAPITAL

SHAFT

BASE

ENTABLATURE

CORINTHIAN

Corinthian. Copyright Encyclopædia Britannica, Inc.; rendering for this edition by Rosen Educational Services

because of the exquisite refinement of the best examples (especially the Parthenon), and partly because it is seen to reflect the emergence in Greece of a rational, philosophical approach to art that replaced earlier belief systems.

There are two types of Greek temple: the Ionic, evolved in Ionia on the eastern shore of the Aegean Sea, and the Doric, evolved on the western shore. The two systems are called orders because their parts and proportions are ordered and coordinated. Their forms must originally have had symbolic meaning. Both show the same basic plan: a central windowless statue chamber, the cella; a porch, usually with two columns in front; and a ring of columns, the peristyle, around the four sides.

The Ionic and Doric temples differ in their details. The Doric temple is simple in plan, the Ionic larger with a double peristyle. The columns differ: the Doric has a dish-shaped top, or capital, and no base, while the Ionic has paired volutes at its capital and carved rings at its base. The lintels, or entablatures, spanning the columns are also distinct, the Doric having a row of projecting blocks, or triglyphs, between sculpted panels called metopes. The Ionic elements are

75

smaller and taller, the Doric forms shorter and broader.

What is remarkable and unique about the Greek temple is the conscious adjustment of these orders by Greek architects for purely aesthetic effect. For the first time in history, architects, not priests, directed these building projects.

MATHEMATICS AND SCIENCE

The Greeks were the first people to develop a truly mathematical spirit. They were interested not only in the applications of mathematics but in its philosophical significance, which was especially appreciated by Plato. Mathematics was also the basis for the first sciences in the modern sense. Thus numerous Greek scholars are recognized for achievements in both fields.

The Greeks developed the idea of using mathematical formulas to prove the validity of a proposition. Some Greeks, like Aristotle, engaged in the theoretical study of logic, the analysis of correct reasoning. No previous mathematics had dealt with abstract entities or the idea of a mathematical proof. Pythagoras provided one of the first proofs in mathematics and discovered irrational

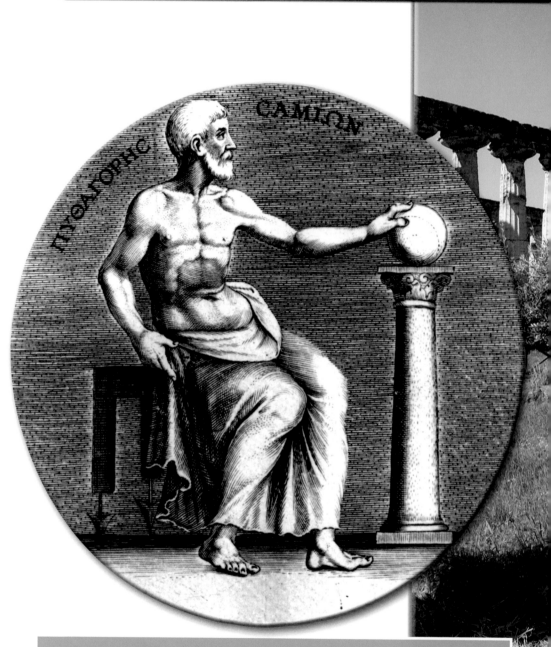

Pythagoras. **Hulton Archive/Getty Images**

numbers. The Pythagorean theorem relates the sides of a right triangle with their corresponding squares.

The three greatest mathematicians of antiquity were Euclid, Apollonius of Perga, and Archimedes. Euclid's *Elements of Geometry* used logic and deductive reasoning to set up axioms, postulates, and a collection of theorems related to plane and solid geometry, as well as a theory of proportions used to resolve the difficulty of irrational numbers. Apollonius, best known for his work on conic sections, coined the terms "parabola," "hyperbola," and "ellipse." Archimedes was both a great mathematician and an important early writer on the science of mechanics.

Mathematics and mechanics were put to practical use during Greece's golden age. The knowledge of geometry was applied widely in Greek architecture. The knowledge of physics was used in building as well as in war. The lever made it possible to move huge stones for building. With the catapult soldiers were able to hurl heavy spears or large rocks at enemy fortifications.

Another science that the ancient Greeks helped to develop was astronomy. They could foretell to the day when a certain planet would be visible and even where it would appear in the heavens. This kind of science was what would be known today as the "astronomy of position." The most influential ancient astronomer was Ptolemy, who lived in Alexandria in the 2nd century AD. He proposed that Earth was at the center of the universe, a theory that persisted until the 16th century.

Theoretical science began when the Greeks started to ask serious questions about the world around them. They wanted to know what things were made of and where they came from. They wished not only to make and build things but to know how and why things were as they were. Asking these questions and getting the first answers—even if some of these answers were later proved wrong—laid the foundations of Western science.

CONCLUSION

The Hellenistic Age ended with the establishment of the Roman Empire in 31 BC. However, the influence of the ancient Greeks' endured. The Romans borrowed from the art and science of the Greeks and drew upon their philosophy. As Christianity developed, it was influenced by Greek thought. During the barbarian invasions, Greek learning was preserved by Christians in Constantinople and Muslims in Cairo. Its light shone again in the Middle Ages with the founding of the great universities in Italy, France, and England. During the Renaissance it provided an impetus for the rebirth of art and literature. Modern science rests on the Greek idea of humankind's capacity to solve problems by rational methods. And the democracy established in Athens was the model for one of the most important forms of government in history. In almost every phase of life, Greek thought can be seen among the peoples who inherited this legacy.

acropolis The upper fortified part of an ancient Greek city.

agora A gathering place; the marketplace of ancient Greek cities.

armada A fleet of warships.

city-state An autonomous state consisting of a city and surrounding territory.

coffers Treasury; funds.

demagogue A leader who makes use of popular prejudices and false claims and promises in order to gain power.

draconic Of, relating to, or characteristic of Draco or the severe code of laws framed by him.

enmity Positive, active, and typically mutual hatred or ill will.

eupatridae The hereditary aristocrats of ancient Athens.

frieze A sculptured or richly ornamented band (as on a building).

garrison A military post, especially a permanent military installation.

hellenizein To act like a Greek.

isthmus A narrow strip of land connecting two larger land areas.

lyric A short poem of songlike quality.

metic A resident alien in ancient Greece, including slaves.

oligarchy A government of the few, in which a small group of people exercises control over everyone else.

pediment A triangular space that forms the gable of a low-pitched roof and that is usually filled with relief sculpture in classical architecture.

pentathlon A five-part event at the Olympics of ancient Greece that included running, wrestling, jumping, and throwing the discus and javelin.

peristyle A series of columns surrounding a building or court.

polis An ancient Greek city-state.

postulate A hypothesis advanced as an essential presupposition, condition, or premise of a line of reasoning .

strategos A general in ancient Greece, often functioning as a state officer with wider duties.

treatise A systemic exposition or argument in writing including a methodical discussion of the facts and principles involved and conclusions reached.

vitality Physical vigor.

Archaeological Institute of America
656 Beacon Street, 6th Floor
Boston, MA 02215-2006
(718) 472-3050
Web site: http://www.archaeological.org
The Archaeological Institute of America
   promotes public interest in the cultures
   of the past, supports archaeological
   research, fosters the practice of archae-
   ology, advocates the preservation of the
   world's archaeological heritage, and represents the discipline in the wider world.

The British Museum: Ancient Greece
Great Russell Street
London, WC1B 3DG
United Kingdom
+44 (0) 20 7323 8299
Web site: http://www.ancientgreece.co.uk
The British Museum is a museum located in
   London that has been open since the late
   18th century. It features an extensive exhibit
   on the culture and history of ancient Greece.

Department of History and Classics
2-28 Henry Marshall Tory Building
University of Alberta
Edmonton, AB T6G 2H4
Canada

(780) 492-3270

Web site: http://www.uofaweb.ualberta.ca/ historyandclassics

The Department of History and Classics at the University of Alberta offers information about ancient Greece and its history and culture.

Department of Greek and Roman Classics
Temple University
1114 West Berks Street
Philadelphia, PA 19122
(215) 204-8267

Web site: http://www.temple.edu/classics

The Department of Greek and Roman classics at Temple University provides a wealth of information about the study of ancient Greece, including links to further Web resources.

WEB SITES

Due to the changing nature of Internet links, Rosen Educational Services has developed an online list of Web sites related to the subject of this book. This site is updated regularly. Please use this link to access the list:

http://www.rosenlinks.com/

Belozerskaya, Marina, and Lapatin, Kenneth. *Ancient Greece: Art, Architecture, and History* (J. Paul Getty Museum, 2004).

Connolly, Peter. *Ancient Greece* (Oxford Univ. Press, 2001).

Day, Nancy. *Your Travel Guide to Ancient Greece* (Runestone Press, 2001).

Evslin, Bernard. *Heroes, Gods and Monsters of the Greek Myths* (Dell Laurel-Leaf, 2005).

Lassieur, Allison. *The Ancient Greeks* (Franklin Watts, 2004).

Malam, John, and Bergin, Mark. *An Ancient Greek Temple* (Book House, 2008).

Nardo, Don. *Philosophy and Science in Ancient Greece: The Pursuit of Knowledge* (Lucent, 2004).

Pearson, Anne. *Ancient Greece* (DK Publishing, 2007).

Villing, Alexandra. *The Ancient Greeks: Their Lives and Their World* (J. Paul Getty Museum, 2010).

Wright, Anne. *Inside Ancient Greece: Philosophy and Writing* (M.E. Sharpe, 2008).

INDEX

31-70

7/24/12.

LONGWOOD PUBLIC LIBRARY
800 Middle Country Road
Middle Island, NY 11953
(631) 924-6400
mylpl.net

LIBRARY HOURS

Monday-Friday	9:30 a.m. - 9:00 p.m.
Saturday	9:30 a.m. - 5:00 p.m.
Sunday (Sept-June)	1:00 p.m. - 5:00 p.m.